Lawn Care Small Business Startup book

Secrets to discount startup business supplies, fundraising & expert home business plan.

by Brian Mahoney

TABLE OF CONTENTS

DEDICATION

This book is dedicated to Mark Cammack
A blessing from God and a good friend.

ACKNOWLEDGMENTS

I WOULD LIKE TO ACKNOWLEDGE ALL THE HARD WORK OF THE MEN AND WOMEN OF THE UNITED STATES MILITARY, WHO RISK THEIR LIVES ON A DAILY BASIS, TO MAKE THE WORLD A SAFER PLACE.

Disclaimer

This book was written as a guide to starting a business. As with any other high yielding action, starting a business has a certain degree of risk. This book is not meant to take the place of accounting, legal, financial or other professional advice. If advice is needed in any of these fields, you are advised to seek the services of a professional.

While the author has attempted to make the information in this book as accurate as possible, no guarantee is given as to the accuracy or currency of any individual item. Laws and procedures related to business are constantly changing.

Therefore, in no event shall Brian Mahoney or MahoneyProducts Publishers be liable for any special, indirect, or consequential damages or any damages whatsoever in connection with the use of the information herein provided.

Lawn Care
Business

LAWN CARE BUSINESS OVERVIEW

LAWN CARE BUSINESS

Estimated Yearly Income: $25,000-$50,000

Startup Costs: $200-$1,500

Normal fees: $15-$20 per hour or flat rate of $50-$100 per job.

Marketing/Advertising: Organic SEO, YouTube, Google Ads, Flyers on front doors, Zero Cost Online Marketing, Internet Marketing, Business Cards, Classified Ads, Yellow Pages, Online Yellow Pages,Referrals, Direct Mail Postcards, Business Groups, business website

Start up Equipment: Power mower, rakes, leaf blower, power trimmer and spreader, pickup truck or station wagon

Skills needed: Lawn care knowledge, stamina

Home Based: Can be operated from home.

Part Time: Can be operated part-time.

Hidden Costs:

Insurance & licensing; Travel Expenses, Equipment rental

LAWN CARE BUSINESS

What Lawn Care Workers Do

Lawn Care workers

Lawn Care workers ensure that the grounds of houses, businesses, parks, and urban infrastructure are attractive, orderly, and healthy in order to provide a pleasant outdoor environment.

Duties

Lawn Care workers typically do the following:

Mow, edge, and fertilize lawns

Weed and mulch landscape beds

Trim hedges, shrubs, and small trees

Remove dead, damaged, or unwanted trees

Plant flowers, trees, and shrubs

Water lawns, landscapes, and gardens

Monitor and maintain plant health

Lawn Care workers are generally under the direction of a professional grounds manager and perform a variety of tasks to achieve a pleasant and functional outdoor environment. They also care for indoor gardens and plants in commercial and public facilities, such as malls, hotels, and botanical gardens.

LAWN CARE BUSINESS

The following are examples of types of Lawn Care workers:

Landscaping workers plant trees, flowers, and shrubs to create new outdoor spaces or upgrade existing ones. They also trim, fertilize, mulch, and water plants. Some grade and install lawns or construct hardscapes such as walkways, patios, and decks. Others help install lighting or sprinkler systems. Landscaping workers are employed in a variety of residential and commercial settings, such as homes, apartment buildings, office buildings, shopping malls, and hotels and motels.

Groundskeeping workers, also called groundskeepers, maintain grounds. They care for plants and trees, rake and mulch leaves, and clear snow from walkways. They work on athletic fields, golf courses, cemeteries, university campuses, and parks, as well as in many of the same settings that landscaping workers work. They also see to the proper upkeep of sidewalks, parking lots, fountains, fences, planters, and benches, as well as groundskeeping equipment.

Groundskeeping workers who care for athletic fields keep natural and artificial turf in top condition, mark out boundaries, and paint turf with team logos and names before events. They mow, water, fertilize, and aerate the fields regularly. They must ensure that the underlying soil on fields with natural turf has the composition required to allow proper drainage and to support the grass used on the field. In sports venues, they vacuum and disinfect synthetic turf to prevent the growth of harmful bacteria and they remove the turf and replace the cushioning pad periodically.

LAWN CARE BUSINESS

Tree trimmers and pruners, also called arborists, cut away dead or excess branches from trees or shrubs to clear utility lines, roads, and sidewalks. Many of these workers strive to improve the appearance and health of trees and plants, and some specialize in diagnosing and treating tree diseases. Others specialize in pruning, trimming, and shaping ornamental trees and shrubs. Tree trimmers and pruners use chain saws, chippers, and stump grinders while on the job. When trimming near power lines, they usually work on truck-mounted lifts and use power pruners.

How to Become a Lawn Care Worker

Some workers obtain a degree in landscape design or horticulture.

Most Lawn Care workers need no formal education and are trained on the job. Most states require licensing for workers who apply pesticides and fertilizers.

Education

Although most Lawn Care jobs have no education requirements, some employers may require formal education or certification in areas such as landscape design, horticulture, or arboriculture.

Licenses, Certifications, and Registrations

LAWN CARE BUSINESS

Most states require workers who apply pesticides and fertilizers to be licensed. Obtaining a license usually involves passing a test on the proper use and disposal of insecticides, herbicides, and fungicides.

Although professional certification is not required, it can demonstrate competency and reliability for prospective clients and employers.

The National Association of Landscape Professionals offers seven certifications in landscaping and Lawn Care for workers at various experience levels.

The Tree Care Industry Association offers certification for tree care safety professionals.

The International Society of Arboriculture offers six certifications for workers at various experience levels.

The Professional Grounds Management Society offers certification for workers at various experience levels.

Training

LAWN CARE BUSINESS

A short period of on-the-job training is usually enough to teach new hires the skills they need, which often include how to plant and maintain areas and how to use mowers, trimmers, leaf blowers, small tractors, and other equipment. Large institutional employers such as golf courses, university campuses, or municipalities may supplement on-the-job training with coursework in horticulture, arboriculture, urban forestry, insect and disease diagnosis, tree climbing, or small-engine repair.

Important Qualities

Physical stamina. Lawn Care workers must be capable of doing physically strenuous labor for long hours, occasionally in extreme heat or cold.

Self-motivated. Because they often work with little supervision, Lawn Care workers must be able to do their job independently.

Visualization. Lawn Care workers must have the ability to imagine how plants, trees, shrubs, and other landscaping will look before planting or trimming.

LAWN CARE BUSINESS

Pay

The median hourly wage for Lawn Care workers was $14.85 in May 2019. The median wage is the wage at which half the workers in an occupation earned more than that amount and half earned less. The lowest 10 percent earned less than $10.53, and the highest 10 percent earned more than $23.18.

Median hourly wages for Lawn Care workers in May 2019 were as follows:

Tree trimmers and pruners $19.22

Pesticide handlers, sprayers,

and applicators, vegetation   17.23

Lawn Care workers, all other   15.43

Landscaping and groundskeeping workers   14.63

In May 2019, the median hourly wages for Lawn Care workers in the top industries in which they worked were as follows:

LAWN CARE BUSINESS

Educational services; state, local, and private $16.39

Government   15.10

Services to buildings and dwellings   15.09

Amusement, gambling, and recreation industries   12.84

Many Lawn Care jobs are seasonal. Jobs are most common in the spring, summer, and fall, when planting, mowing, and trimming are most frequent. However, many also provide other seasonal services, such as snow removal and installation and removal of holiday décor.

LAWN CARE Wholesale Web Rolodex

Lawn Care Equipment

http://www.equipmenttraderonline.com/

http://www.libertydiscount.com/

http://www.wholesaledistributorsnet.com/garden.html

https://gsaauctions.gov/gsaauctions/gsaauctions/

http://www.lawncareequipmentco.com/

http://www.liquidation.com/general-merchandise/wholesale-lawn.html

https://www.alibaba.com/showroom/lawn-mowers-wholesale.html

http://www.powerequipmentdirect.com/

http://www.lawnsite.com/

How to get Free Money for Small Business Start up

https://www.amazon.com/dp/1951929144   Paperback

https://urlzs.com/ZamJw   AudioBook

Chapter 2

How to get started step by step

HOW TO GET STARTED STEP BY STEP

Starting a business involves planning, making key financial decisions and completing a series of legal activities. These 12 easy steps can help you plan, prepare and manage your business.

Step 1: Write a Business Plan

Use these tools and resources to create a business plan. This written guide will help you map out how you will start and run your business successfully.

Step 2: Get Business Assistance and Training

Take advantage of free training and counseling services, from preparing a business plan and securing financing, to expanding or relocating a business from the Small Business Administration.

Step 3: Choose a Business Location

Get advice on how to select a customer-friendly location and comply with zoning laws.

HOW TO GET STARTED STEP BY STEP

Step 4: Finance Your Business

Find government backed loans, venture capital and research grants to help you get started.

Step 5: Determine the Legal Structure of Your Business
Decide which form of ownership is best for you: sole proprietorship, partnership, Limited Liability Company (LLC), corporation, S corporation, nonprofit or cooperative.

Step 6: Register a Business Name ("Doing Business As")
Register your business name with your state government.

Step 7: Get a Tax Identification Number

Learn which tax identification number you'll need to obtain from the IRS and your state revenue agency.

Step 8: Register for State and Local Taxes

Register with your state to obtain a tax identification number, workers' compensation, unemployment and disability insurance.

HOW TO GET STARTED STEP BY STEP

Step 9: Obtain Business Licenses and Permits

Get a list of federal, state and local licenses and permits required for your business.

Step 10: Understand Employer Responsibilities

Learn the legal steps you need to take to hire employees.

Step 11: Get Equipment and Supplies

Get everything together that you'll need in order to actually operate. This includes items such as a truck, chemicals, equipment, and the various business forms such as service contracts. Once you have these things together, you can start the marketing process in order to get new customers.

Step 12: Your Marketing Plan

Coming up with your overall marketing plan, and implementing that plan. When you're just starting, it is usually best to choose one or two major marketing strategies, and work on those until you're getting a steady stream of customers. Once you've gotten good at once specific marketing avenue, then it's a good idea to move on to another one, and repeat the process. You can begin with "Zero cost marketing" and scale up once you are bringing in constant sales.

Chapter 3

How to Write a Business Plan

How to Write a Business Plan

Millions of people want to know what is the secret to making money. Most have come to the conclusion that it is to start a business. So how to start a business? The first thing you do to start is business is to create a business plan.

A business plan is a formal statement of a set of business goals, the reasons they are believed attainable, and the plan for reaching those goals. It may also contain background information about the organization or team attempting to reach those goals.

A professional business plan consists of ten parts.

1. Executive Summary

The executive summary is often considered the most important section of a business plan. This section briefly tells your reader where your company is, where you want to take it, and why your business idea will be successful. If you are seeking financing, the executive summary is also your first opportunity to grab a potential investor's interest.

How to Write a Business Plan

2. Company Description

This section of your plan provides a high-level review of the different elements of your business. This is akin to an extended elevator pitch and can help readers and potential investors quickly understand the goal of your business and its unique proposition.

3. Market Analysis

The market analysis section of your plan should illustrate your industry and market knowledge as well as any of your research findings and conclusions. This section is usually presented after the company description.

4. Organization and Management

Organization and Management follows the Market Analysis. This section should include: your company's organizational structure, details about the ownership of your company, profiles of your management team, and the qualifications of your board of directors.

5. Service or Product Line

Once you've completed the Organizational and Management section of your plan, the next part of your plan is where you describe your service or product, emphasizing the benefits to potential and current customers. Focus on why your particular product will fill a need for your target customers.

6. Marketing and Sales

Once you've completed the Service or Product Line section of your plan, the next part of your plan should focus on your marketing and sales management strategy for your business.

7. Funding Request

If you are seeking funding for your business venture, use this section to outline your requirements.

How to Write a Business Plan

8. Financial Projections

You should develop the Financial Projections section after you've analyzed the market and set clear objectives. That's when you can allocate resources efficiently. The following is a list of the critical financial statements to include in your business plan packet.

9. Marketing and Sales

Once you've completed the Service or Product Line section of your plan, the next part of your business plan should focus on your marketing and sales management strategy for your business.

10. Appendix

The Appendix should be provided to readers on an as-needed basis. In other words, it should not be included with the main body of your business plan. Your plan is your communication tool; as such, it will be seen by a lot of people. Some of the information in the business section you will not want everyone to see, but specific individuals (such as creditors) may want access to this information to make lending decisions. Therefore, it is important to have the appendix within easy reach.

How to Write a Business Plan

How to make your business plan stand out.

One of the first steps to business planning is determining your target market and why they would want to buy from you.

For example, is the market you serve the best one for your product or service? Are the benefits of dealing with your business clear and are they aligned with customer needs? If you're unsure about the answers to any of these questions, take a step back and revisit the foundation of your business plan.

The following tips can help you clarify what your business has to offer, identify the right target market for it and build a niche for yourself.

Chapter 4

FREE MONEY TO GET STARTED

FREE MONEY TO GET STARTED

Government grants. Many people either don't believe government grants exsist or they don't think they would ever be able to get government grant money.

First lets make one thing clear. Government grant money is **YOUR MONEY**. Government money comes from taxes paid by residents of this country. Depending on what state you live in, you are paying taxes on almost everything....Property tax for your house. Property tax on your car. Taxes on the things you purchase in the mall, or at the gas station. Taxes on your gasoline, the food you buy etc.

So get yourself in the frame of mind that you are not a charity case or too proud to ask for help, because billionaire companies like GM, Big Banks and most of Corporate America is not hesitating to get their share of **YOUR MONEY**!

There are over two thousand three hundred (2,300) Federal Government Assistance Programs. Some are loans but many are formula grants and project grants. To see all of the programs available go to:

http://www.CFDA.gov

FREE MONEY TO GET STARTED

WRITING A GRANT PROPOSAL

The Basic Components of a Proposal

There are eight basic components to creating a solid proposal package:

(1) The proposal summary;

(2)   Introduction of organization;

(3)   The problem statement

         (or needs assessment);

(4)   Project objectives;

(5)   Project methods or design;

(6)   Project evaluation;

(7)   Future funding; and

(8)   The project budget.

FREE MONEY TO GET STARTED

The following will provide an overview of these components.

1. The Proposal Summary: Outline of Project Goals

The proposal summary outlines the proposed project and should appear at the beginning of the proposal. It could be in the form of a cover letter or a separate page,

but should definitely be brief -- no longer than two or three paragraphs. The summary would be most useful if it were prepared after the proposal has been developed in order to encompass all the key summary points necessary to communicate the objectives of the project. It is this document that becomes the cornerstone of your proposal, and the initial impression it gives will be critical to the success of your venture. In many cases, the summary will be the first part of the proposal package seen by agency officials and very possibly could be the only part of the package that is carefully reviewed before the decision is made to consider the project any further.

FREE MONEY TO GET STARTED

The applicant must select a fundable project which can be supported in view of the local need. Alternatives, in the absence of Federal support, should be pointed out. The influence of the project both during and after the project period should be explained. The consequences of the project as a result of funding should be highlighted.

2. Introduction: Presenting a Credible Applicant or Organization

The applicant should gather data about its organization from all available sources. Most proposals require a description of an applicant's organization to describe its past and present operations. Some features to consider are:

A brief biography of board members and key staff members.

The organization's goals, philosophy, track record with other grantors, and any success stories.

The data should be relevant to the goals of the Federal grantor agency and should establish the applicant's credibility.

FREE MONEY TO GET STARTED

3. The Problem Statement: Stating the Purpose at Hand

The problem statement (or needs assessment) is a key element of a proposal that makes a clear, concise, and well-supported statement of the problem to be addressed. The best way to collect information about the problem is to conduct and document both a formal and informal needs assessment for a program in the FF-4 11-08 target or service area. The information provided should be both factual and directly related to the problem addressed by the proposal. Areas to document are:

The purpose for developing the proposal.

The beneficiaries -- who are they and how will they benefit.

The social and economic costs to be affected.

The nature of the problem (provide as much hard evidence as possible).

How the applicant organization came to realize the problem exists, and what is currently being done about the problem.

FREE MONEY TO GET STARTED

The remaining alternatives available when funding has been exhausted. Explain what will happen to the project and the impending implications.

Most importantly, the specific manner through which problems might be solved. Review the resources needed, considering how they will be used and to what end.

There is a considerable body of literature on the exact assessment techniques to be used. Any local, regional, or State government planning office, or local university offering course work in planning and evaluation techniques should be able to provide excellent background references. Types of data that may be collected include: historical, geographic, quantitative, factual, statistical, and philosophical information, as well as studies completed by colleges, and literature searches from public or university libraries. Local colleges or universities which have a department or section related to the proposal topic may help determine if there is interest in developing a student or faculty project to conduct a needs assessment. It may be helpful to include examples of the findings for highlighting in the proposal.

FREE MONEY TO GET STARTED

4. Project Objectives: Goals and Desired Outcome

Program objectives refer to specific activities in a proposal. It is necessary to identify all objectives related to the goals to be reached, and the methods to be employed to achieve the stated objectives. Consider quantities or things measurable and refer to a problem statement and the outcome of proposed activities when developing a well-stated objective. The figures used should be verifiable. Remember, if the proposal is funded, the stated objectives will probably be used to evaluate program progress, so be realistic. There is literature available to help identify and write program objectives.

5. Program Methods and Program Design: A Plan of Action

The program design refers to how the project is expected to work and solve the stated problem. Sketch out the following:

The activities to occur along with the related resources and staff needed to operate the project(inputs).

A flow chart of the organizational features of the project. Describe how the parts interrelate, where personnel will be needed, and what they are expected to do. Identify the kinds of facilities, transportation, and support services required (throughputs).

FREE MONEY TO GET STARTED

Explain what will be achieved through 1 and 2 above (outputs); i.e., plan for measurable results. Project staff may be required to produce evidence of program performance through an examination of stated objectives during either a site visit by the Federal grantor agency and or grant reviews which may involve peer review committees.

It may be useful to devise a diagram of the program design. For example, draw a three column block. Each column is headed by one of the parts (inputs, throughputs and outputs), and on the left 11-08 FF-5 (next to the first column) specific program features should be identified (i.e., implementation, staffing, procurement, and systems development).

In the grid, specify something about the program design, for example, assume the first column is labeled inputs and the first row is labeled staff. On the grid one might specify under inputs five nurses to operate a child care unit. The throughput might be to maintain charts, counsel the children, and set up a daily routine; outputs might be to discharge 25 healthy children per week. This type of procedure will help to conceptualize both the scope and detail of the project.

FREE MONEY TO GET STARTED

Wherever possible, justify in the narrative the course of action taken. The most economical method should be used that does not compromise or sacrifice project quality. The financial expenses associated with performance of the project will later become points of negotiation with the Federal program staff. If everything is not carefully justified in writing in the proposal, after negotiation with the Federal grantor agencies, the approved project may resemble less of the original concept. Carefully consider the pressures of the proposed implementation, that is, the time and money needed to acquire each part of the plan. A Program Evaluation and Review Technique (PERT) chart could be useful and supportive in justifying some proposals.

The remaining alternatives available when funding has been exhausted. Explain what will happen to the project and the impending implications.

Highlight the innovative features of the proposal which could be considered distinct from other proposals under consideration.

Whenever possible, use appendices to provide details, supplementary data, references, and information requiring in-depth analysis. These types of data, although supportive of the proposal, if included in the body of the design, could detract from its readability.

Appendices provide the proposal reader with immediate access to details if and when clarification of an idea, sequence or conclusion is required. Time tables, work plans, schedules, activities, methodologies, legal papers, personal vitae, letters of support, and endorsements are examples of appendices.

6. Evaluation: Product and Process Analysis

The evaluation component is two-fold: (1) product evaluation; and (2) process evaluation. Product evaluation addresses results that can be attributed to the project, as well as the extent to which the project has satisfied its desired objectives. Process evaluation addresses how the project was conducted, in terms of consistency with the stated plan of action and the effectiveness of the various activities within the plan.

Most Federal agencies now require some form of program evaluation among grantees. The requirements of the proposed project should be explored carefully. Evaluations may be conducted by an internal staff member, an evaluation firm or both. The applicant should state the amount of time needed to evaluate, how the feedback will be distributed among the proposed staff, and a schedule for review and comment for this type of communication.

FREE MONEY TO GET STARTED

Evaluation designs may start at the beginning, middle or end of a project, but the applicant should specify a start-up time. It is practical to submit an evaluation design at the start of a project for two reasons:

Convincing evaluations require the collection of appropriate data before and during program operations; and,

If the evaluation design cannot be prepared at the outset then a critical review of the program design may be advisable.

Even if the evaluation design has to be revised as the project progresses, it is much easier and cheaper to modify a good design. If the problem is not well defined and carefully analyzed for cause and effect relationships then a good evaluation design may be difficult to achieve. Sometimes a pilot study is needed to begin the identification of facts and relationships. Often a thorough literature search may be sufficient.

FREE MONEY TO GET STARTED

Evaluation requires both coordination and agreement among program decision makers (if known). Above all, the Federal grantor agency's requirements should be highlighted in the evaluation design. Also, Federal grantor agencies may require specific evaluation techniques such as designated data formats (an existing FF-6 11-08 information collection system) or they may offer financial inducements for voluntary participation in a national evaluation study. The applicant should ask specifically about these points. Also, consult the Criteria For Selecting Proposals section of the Catalog program description to determine the exact evaluation methods to be required for the program if funded.

7. Future Funding: Long-Term Project Planning

Describe a plan for continuation beyond the grant period, and/or the availability of other resources necessary to implement the grant. Discuss maintenance and future program funding if program is for construction activity. Account for other needed expenditures if program includes purchase of equipment.

FREE MONEY TO GET STARTED

8.The Proposal Budget: Planning the Budget

Funding levels in Federal assistance programs change yearly. It is useful to review the appropriations over the past several years to try to project future funding levels (see Financial Information section of the Catalog program description).

However, it is safer to never anticipate that the income from the grant will be the sole support for the project. This consideration should be given to the overall budget requirements, and in particular, to budget line items most subject to inflationary pressures. Restraint is important in determining inflationary cost projections (avoid padding budget line items), but attempt to anticipate possible future increases.

Some vulnerable budget areas are: utilities, rental of buildings and equipment, salary increases, food, telephones, insurance, and transportation. Budget adjustments are sometimes made after the grant award, but this can be a lengthy process. Be certain that implementation, continuation and phase-down costs can be met. Consider costs associated with leases, evaluation systems, hard/soft match requirements, audits, development, implementation and maintenance of information and accounting systems, and other long-term financial commitments.

FREE MONEY TO GET STARTED

A well-prepared budget justifies all expenses and is consistent with the proposal narrative. Some areas in need of an evaluation for consistency are:

(1) the salaries in the proposal in relation to those of the applicant organization should be similar;

(2) if new staff persons are being hired, additional space and equipment should be considered, as necessary;

(3) if the budget calls for an equipment purchase, it should be the type allowed by the grantor agency;

(4) if additional space is rented, the increase in insurance should be supported;

(5) if an indirect cost rate applies to the proposal, the division between direct and indirect costs should not be in conflict, and the aggregate budget totals should refer directly to the approved formula; and

(6) if matching costs are required, the contributions to the matching fund should be taken out of the budget unless otherwise specified in the application instructions.

FREE MONEY TO GET STARTED

It is very important to become familiar with Government-wide circular requirements. The Catalog identifies in the program description section

(as information is provided from the agencies)

the particular circulars applicable to a Federal program, and summarizes coordination of Executive Order 12372, "Intergovernmental Review of Programs" requirements in Appendix I. The applicant should thoroughly review the appropriate circulars since they are essential in determining items such as cost principles and conforming with Government guidelines for Federal domestic assistance.

Chapter 5

SBA LOANS

SBA LOANS

General Small Business Loans:

Loan Program, SBA's most common loan program, includes financial help for businesses with special requirements.

Loan Program Eligibility

SBA provides loans to businesses; so the requirements of eligibility are based on specific aspects of the business and its principals. As such, the key factors of eligibility are based on what the business does to receive its income, the character of its ownership and where the business operates.

SBA generally does not specify what businesses are eligible. Rather, the agency outlines what businesses are not eligible. However, there are some universally applicable requirements. To be eligible for assistance, businesses must:

SBA LOANS

Operate for profit

Be small, as defined by SBA

Be engaged in, or propose to do business in, the United States or its possessions

Have reasonable invested equity

Use alternative financial resources, including personal assets, before seeking financial assistance

Be able to demonstrate a need for the loan proceeds

Use the funds for a sound business purpose

Not be delinquent on any existing debt obligations to the U.S. government

Ineligible Businesses

A business must be engaged in an activity SBA determines as acceptable for financial assistance from a federal provider. The following list of businesses types are not eligible for assistance because of the activities they conduct:

SBA LOANS

Financial businesses primarily engaged in the business of lending, such as banks, finance companies, payday lenders, some leasing companies and factors (pawn shops, although engaged in lending, may qualify in some circumstances)

Businesses owned by developers and landlords that do not actively use or occupy the assets acquired or improved with the loan proceeds (except when the property is leased to the business at zero profit for the property's owners)

Life insurance companies

Businesses located in a foreign country (businesses in the U.S. owned by aliens may qualify)

Businesses engaged in pyramid sale distribution plans, where a participant's primary incentive is based on the sales made by an ever-increasing number of participants

Businesses deriving more than one-third of gross annual revenue from legal gambling activities

Businesses engaged in any illegal activity

Private clubs and businesses that limit the number of memberships for reasons other than capacity

SBA LOANS

Government-owned entities

Businesses principally engaged in teaching, instructing, counseling or indoctrinating religion or religious beliefs, whether in a religious or secular setting

Consumer and marketing cooperatives (producer cooperatives are eligible)

Loan packagers earning more than one third of their gross annual revenue from packaging SBA loans

Businesses in which the lender or CDC, or any of its associates owns an equity interest

Businesses that present live performances of an indecent sexual nature or derive directly or indirectly more 2.5 percent of gross revenue through the sale of products or services, or the presentation of any depictions or displays, of an indecent sexual nature

Businesses primarily engaged in political or lobbying activities

Speculative businesses (such as oil exploration)

There are also eligibility factors for financial assistance based on the activities of the owners and the historical operation of the business. As such, the business cannot have been:

SBA LOANS

A business that caused the government to have incurred a loss related to a prior business debt

A business owned 20 percent or more by a person associated with a different business that caused the government to have incurred a loss related to a prior business debt

A business owned 20 percent or more by a person who is incarcerated, on probation, on parole, or has been indicted for a felony or a crime of moral depravity

Special Considerations

Special considerations apply to some types of businesses and individuals, which include:

Franchises are eligible except when a franchiser retains power to control operations to such an extent as to equate to an employment contract; the franchisee must have the right to profit from efforts commensurate with ownership

Recreational facilities and clubs are eligible if the facilities are open to the general public, or in membership-only situations, membership is not selectively denied or restricted to any particular groups

SBA LOANS

Farms and agricultural businesses are eligible, but these applicants should first explore Farm Service Agency (FSA) programs, particularly if the applicant has a prior or existing relationship with FSA

Fishing vessels are eligible, but those seeking funds for the construction or reconditioning of vessels with a cargo capacity of five tons or more must first request financing from the National Marine Fisheries Service

Privately owned medical facilities including hospitals, clinics, emergency outpatient facilities, and medical and dental laboratories are eligible; recovery and nursing homes are also eligible, provided they are licensed by the appropriate government agency and they provide more than room and board

An Eligible Passive Company (EPC) must use loan proceeds to acquire or lease, and/or improve or renovate, real or personal property that it leases to one or more operating companies and must not make any profit from conducting its activities

Legal aliens are eligible; however, consideration is given to status (e.g., resident, lawful temporary resident) in determining the business' degree of risk

Probation or parole: Applications will not be accepted from firms in which a principal is currently incarcerated, on parole, on probation or is a defendant in a criminal proceeding

SBA LOANS

Loan Amounts, Fees & Interest Rates

The specific terms of SBA loans are negotiated between a borrower and an SBA-approved lender. In general, the following provisions apply to all SBA 7(a) loans.

Loan Amounts

7(a) loans have a maximum loan amount of $5 million. SBA does not set a minimum loan amount. The average 7(a) loan amount in fiscal year 2015 was $371,628.

Fees

Loans guaranteed by the SBA are assessed a guarantee fee. This fee is based on the loan's maturity and the dollar amount guaranteed, not the total loan amount.

The lender initially pays the guaranty fee and they have the option to pass that expense on to the borrower at closing. The funds to reimburse the lender can be included in the overall loan proceeds.

SBA LOANS

On loans under $150,000 made after October 1, 2013, the fees will be set at zero percent. On any loan greater than $150,000 with a maturity of one year or shorter, the fee is 0.25 percent of the guaranteed portion of the loan. On loans with maturities of more than one year, the normal fee is 3 percent of the SBA-guaranteed portion on loans of $150,000 to $700,000, and 3.5 percent on loans of more than $700,000. There is also an additional fee of 0.25 percent on any guaranteed portion of more than $1 million.

Interest Rates

The actual interest rate for a 7(a) loan guaranteed by the SBA is negotiated between the applicant and lender and subject to the SBA maximums. Both fixed and variable interest rate structures are available.

The maximum rate is composed of two parts, a base rate and an allowable spread. There are three acceptable base rates (A prime rate published in a daily national newspaper*, London Interbank One Month Prime plus 3 percent and an SBA Peg Rate).

SBA LOANS

Lenders are allowed to add an additional spread to the base rate to arrive at the final rate. For loans with maturities of shorter than seven years, the maximum spread will be no more than 2.25 percent. For loans with maturities of seven years or more, the maximum spread will be 2.75 percent. The spread on loans of less than $50,000 and loans processed through Express procedures have higher maximums.

*All references to the prime rate refer to the base rate in effect on the first business day of the month the loan application is received by the SBA.

Percentage of Guarantee

SBA can guarantee as much as 85 percent on loans of up to $150,000 and 75 percent on loans of more than $150,000. SBA's maximum exposure amount is $3,750,000. Thus, if a business receives an SBA-guaranteed loan for $5 million, the maximum guarantee to the lender will be $3,750,000 or 75%. SBA Express loans have a maximum guarantee set at 50 percent.
7(a) Loan Application Checklist

The specific terms of SBA loans are negotiated between a borrower and an SBA-approved lender. In general, the following provisions apply to all SBA 7(a) loans.

SBA LOANS

Loan Processing Time

There are two 7(a) loan process options with different time frames. In addition to standard procedures, SBA Express processing offers an expedited turnaround.

Special Types of 7(a) Loans

SBA offers several special purpose 7(a) loans to aid businesses that have been impacted by NAFTA, provide financial assistance to Employee Stock Ownership Plans, and help implement pollution controls.

Chapter 6

SBA Microloan Program

SBA Microloan Program

The Microloan program provides loans up to $50,000 to help small businesses and certain not-for-profit childcare centers start up and expand. The average microloan is about $13,000.

The U.S. Small Business Administration provides funds to specially designated intermediary lenders, which are nonprofit community-based organizations with experience in lending as well as management and technical assistance. These intermediaries administer the Microloan program for eligible borrowers.

Eligibility Requirements

Each intermediary lender has its own lending and credit requirements. Generally, intermediaries require some type of collateral as well as the personal guarantee of the business owner.

SBA Microloan Program

Use of Microloan Proceeds

Microloans can be used for:

Working capital

Inventory or supplies

Furniture or fixtures

Machinery or equipment

Proceeds from an SBA microloan cannot be used to pay existing debts or to purchase real estate.

Repayment Terms, Interest Rates, and Fees

Loan repayment terms vary according to several factors:

Loan amount

Planned use of funds

Requirements determined by the intermediary lender

Needs of the small business borrower

SBA Microloan Program

The maximum repayment term allowed for an SBA microloan is six years.

Interest rates vary, depending on the intermediary lender and costs to the intermediary from the U.S. Treasury. Generally, these rates will be between 8 and 13 percent.

Application Process

Microloans are available through certain nonprofit, community-based organizations that are experienced in lending and business management assistance. If you apply for SBA microloan financing, you may be required to fulfill training or planning requirements before your loan application is considered. This business training is designed to help you launch or expand your business.

Find a Microloan Provider

To apply for a Microloan, you must work with an SBA approved intermediary in your area. Approved intermediaries make all credit decisions on SBA microloans. For more information, you can contact your local SBA District Office or view the list of Participating Microloan Intermediary Lenders in the Attachments list below.

Chapter 7

Business Legal Structure

Business Legal Structure

When you are starting a business, one of the first decisions you have to make is the type of business you want to create. A sole proprietorship? A corporation? A limited liability company? This decision is important, because the type of business you create determines the types of applications you’ll need to submit. You should also research liability implications for personal investments you make into your business, as well as the taxes you will need to pay. It’s important to understand each business type and select the one that is best suited for your situation and objectives. Keep in mind that you may need to contact several federal agencies, as well as your state business entity registration office.

Here is a list of the most common ways to structure a business.

An S corporation (sometimes referred to as an S Corp) is a special type of corporation created through an IRS tax election. An eligible domestic corporation can avoid double taxation (once to the corporation and again to the shareholders) by electing to be treated as an S corporation.

A partnership is a single business where two or more people share ownership.

Business Legal Structure

Each partner contributes to all aspects of the business, including money, property, labor or skill. In return, each partner shares in the profits and losses of the business.

A limited liability company is a hybrid type of legal structure that provides the limited liability features of a corporation and the tax efficiencies and operational flexibility of a partnership.

The "owners" of an LLC are referred to as "members." Depending on the state, the members can consist of a single individual (one owner), two or more individuals, corporations or other LLCs.

Corporation (C Corporation)

A corporation (sometimes referred to as a C corporation) is an independent legal entity owned by shareholders. This means that the corporation itself, not the shareholders that own it, is held legally liable for the actions and debts the business incurs.

Business Legal Structure

Corporations are more complex than other business structures because they tend to have costly administrative fees and complex tax and legal requirements. Because of these issues, corporations are generally suggested for established, larger companies with multiple employees.

A cooperative is a business or organization owned by and operated for the benefit of those using its services. Profits and earnings generated by the cooperative are distributed among the members, also known as user-owners.

Typically, an elected board of directors and officers run the cooperative while regular members have voting power to control the direction of the cooperative. Members can become part of the cooperative by purchasing shares, though the amount of shares they hold does not affect the weight of their vote.

Chapter 8

Selecting The Right Business Name

Selecting The Right Business Name

Ask 500 people already in business how they decided upon their business name and you will get 500 different answers. Everyone has a story behind how they chose their own business name. Even if the business is named after their own birth name, there's a reason why this was done.

When you open a business, in a sense, you are causing a new birth to begin. This new birth was created from an idea alone by you or your associates. It will have its own bank account, it's own federal identification number, it's own credit accounts, it's own income and it's own bills. On paper, it is another individual! Just as if you were choosing a name for your own unborn child, you need to spend considerable time in deciding upon your business name.

There are several reasons why a good business name is vitally important to your business. The first obvious reason is because it is the initial identification to your customers. No one would want to do business with someone if they didn't have a company name yet.

This makes you look like an amateur who is very unreliable. Even if you call your company "Kevin's Lawn Service," a company name has been established and you are indeed a company. People will therefore feel more comfortable dealing with you.

Selecting The Right Business Name

Secondly, a business name normally is an indication as to the product or service you offer. "Mary's Typing Service," "Karate Club for Men," "Jim-Dandy Jack-of-all-Trades," "Laurie and Steve's Laundry," "Misty's Gift Boutique," and "Star 1 Publishers" are all examples of simple business names that immediately tell the customer what product you offer.

However, most people will choose the simple approach when naming their business. They use their name, their spouse's name, their children's names or a combination of these names when naming a business. The national hamburger-restaurant chain "Wendy's" was named after the owner's daughter.

However, research has proven that these "cutesy" names are not the best names to use for a business. Many experts claim that it makes the business look too "mom-and-pop-sie." However, this depends on the business. If you are selling something that demands this mood or theme to appeal to your market, it's best to use this approach.

Selecting The Right Business Name

Personally, I am inclined to name my businesses with catchy names that stick in people's heads after we have initially made contact. Names like, "Sensible Solutions," "Direct Defenders," "Moonlighters Ink," "Printer's Friend," "Strictly Class," "Collections and Treasures," and "Starlight on Twilight" are all good examples of catchy names. These types of names relate to your product or service but serve as a type of slogan for your business. This is a big help when marketing.

A friend I know owns a business called "Mint and Pepper." He grows and sells his own line of raw seasonings to people in the local area. At a get-together for small businesses, he passed out his business card. The card had a peppermint candy glued on the back and the slogan read: "Your business is worth a mint to us." This marketing concept not only got my friend noticed and remembered, but brought in several large orders for the business.

When you name a child, you may not decide upon a definite name until after they are born. You do this because a name is sometimes associated with a type of personality. When you name a business you may need to wait until you have a product or service to sell and then decide upon a business name before going into the business itself because your business name should give some clue as to what product or service you are selling.

Selecting The Right Business Name

A business named "Joe's Collections" normally wouldn't sell car parts and a business named "Charlie Horse" would not sell knitting supplies.

To generate ideas - begin looking at business signs everywhere you go. Notice which ones catch your eye and stick in your mind. Try and figure out "why" they stuck in your mind. Naturally, the business "Dominos Pizza" sticks in your mind because it is nationally known. These don't count!

Look around and notice the smaller businesses. Take your time. Within a few days you should be able to come up with a few potential business names.

Then, when you finally find a few names you really like - try reciting them to other people and get their opinion. It won't be long until your business will have the proper name that will carry it through it's life!

HINT:

Try to avoid very long names so they will fit into small display ads. Amalgamated International Enterprises can be easily presented as AIE - which is easier and shorter to spell.

Selecting The Right Business Name

Register Your Business Name

Naming your business is an important branding exercise, but if you choose to name your business as anything other than your own personal name then you'll need to register it with the appropriate authorities.

This process is known as registering your "Doing Business As" (DBA) name.

What is a "Doing Business As" Name?

A fictitious name (or assumed name, trade name or DBA name) is a business name that is different from your personal name, the names of your partners or the officially registered name of your LLC or corporation.

It's important to note that when you form a business, the legal name of the business defaults to the name of the person or entity that owns the business, unless you choose to rename it and register it as a DBA name.

For example, consider this scenario: John Smith sets up a painting business. Rather than operate under his own name, John instead chooses to name his business: "John Smith Painting".

This name is considered an assumed name and John will need to register it with the appropriate local government agency.

Selecting The Right Business Name

The legal name of your business is required on all government forms and applications, including your application for employer tax IDs, licenses and permits.

Do I Need a "Doing Business As" Name?

A DBA is needed in the following scenarios:

Sole Proprietors or Partnerships – If you wish to start a business under anything other than your real name, you'll need to register a DBA so that you can do business as another name.

Existing Corporations or LLCs – If your business is already set up and you want to do business under a name other than your existing corporation or LLC name, you will need to register a DBA.

Note: Not all states require the registering of fictitious business names or DBAs.

How to Register your "Doing Business As" Name

Registering your DBA is done either with your county clerk's office or with your state government, depending on where your business is located. There are a few states that do not require the registering of fictitious business names.

Chapter 9

Business
Tax Advantages

Business Tax Advantages

Every year, several thousand people develop an interest in "going into business." Many of these people have an idea, a product or a service they hope to promote into an income producing business
which they can operate from their homes.

If you are one of these people, here are some practical thoughts to consider before hanging out the "Open for Business" sign.

In areas zoned "Residential Only," your proposed business could be illegal. In many areas, zoning restrictions rule out home businesses involving the coming and going of many customers,clients or employees. Many businesses that sell or even store
anything for sale on the premises also fall into this category.

Be sure to check with your local zoning office to see how the ordinances in your particular area may affect your business plans. You may need a special permit to operate your business from your home; and you may find that making small changes in your plan will put you into the position of meeting zoning
standards.

Business Tax Advantages

Many communities grant home occupation permits for businesses involve typing, sewing, and teaching, but turn thumbs down on requests from photographers, interior decorators and home
improvement businesses to be run from the home. And often, even if you are permitted to use your home for a given business, there will be restrictions that you may need to take into consideration. By all means, work with your zoning people, and save yourself time, trouble and dollars.

One of the requirements imposed might be off street parking for your customers or patrons. And, signs are generally forbidden in residential districts. If you teach, there is almost always a limit on the number of students you may have at any one time.

Obtaining zoning approval for your business, then, could be as simple as filling out an application, or it could involve a public hearing. The important points the zoning officials will consider will center around how your business will affect the neighborhood. Will it increase the traffic noticeably on your street? Will there be a substantial increase in noise? And how
will your neighbors feel about this business alongside their homes?

To repeat, check into the zoning restrictions, and then check again to determine if you will need a city license. If you're selling something, you may need a vendor's license, and be required to collect sales taxes on your transactions. The sale tax requirement would result in the need for careful record keeping.

Business Tax Advantages

Licensing can be an involved process, and depending upon the type of business, it could even involve the inspection of your home to determine if it meets with local health and building and fire codes. Should this be the case, you will need to bring your facilities up to the local standards. Usually this will involve some simple repairs or adjustments that you can either do
personally, or hire out to a handyman at a nominal cost.

Still more items to consider: Will your homeowner's insurance cover the property and liability in your new business? This must definitely be resolved, so be sure to talk it over with your insurance agent.

Tax deductions, which were once one of the beauties of engaging in a home business, are not what they once were. To be eligible for business related deductions today, you must use that part of your home claimed EXCLUSIVELY AND REGULARLY as either the principal location of your business, or place reserved to meet patients, clients or customers.

An interesting case in point: if you use your den or a spare bedroom as the principal place of business, working there from 8:00 to 5:00 every day, but permit your children to watch TV in that room during evening hours, the IRS dictates that you cannot
claim a deduction for that room as your office or place of business.

Business Tax Advantages

There are, however, a couple of exceptions to the "exclusive use" rule. One is the storage on inventory in your home, where your home is the location of your trade or business, and your trade or business is the selling of products at retail or wholesale.

According to the IRS, such storage space must be used on a REGULAR Basis, and be separately identifiable space.

Another exception applies to daycare services that are provided for children, the elderly, or physically or mentally handicapped. This exception applies only if the owner of the facility complies with the state laws for licensing.

To be eligible for business deductions, your business must be an activity undertaken with the intent of making profit. It's presumed you meet this requirement if your business makes a profit in any two years of a five-year period.

Once you are this far along, you can deduct business expenses such as supplies, subscriptions to professional journals, and an allowance for the business use of your car or truck. You can also
claim deductions for home related business expenses such as utilities, and in some cases, even a new paint job for your home.

The IRS is going to treat the part of your home you use for business as though it were a separate piece of property. This means that you'll have to keep good records and take care not to mix business and personal matters. No specific method of record
keeping is required, but your records must clearly justify and deductions you claim.

Business Tax Advantages

You can begin by calculating what percentage of the house is used for business, Either by number of rooms or by area in square footage. Thus, if you use one of the five rooms for your business, the business portion is 20 percent. If you run your business out of a room that's 10 by 12 feet, and the total area
of your home is 1,200 square feet, the business space factor is 10 percent.

An extra computation is required if your business is a home day care center. This is one of the exempted activities in which the exclusive use rule doesn't apply. Check with your tax preparer and the IRS for an exact determination.

If you're a renter, you can deduct the part of your rent which is attributable to the business share of your house or apartment. Homeowners can take a deduction based on the depreciation of the
business portion of their house.

There is a limit to the amount you can deduct. This is the amount equal to the gross income generated by the business, minus those home expenses you could deduct even if you weren't operating a business from your home. As an example, real estate taxes and
mortgage interest are deductible regardless of any business Activity in your home, so you must subtract from your business Gross income the percentage that's allocable to the business portion of your home. You thus arrive at the maximum amount for home-related business deductions.

Business Tax Advantages

If you are self-employed, you claim your business deductions on SCHEDULE C, PROFIT(or LOSS) for BUSINESS OR PROFESSION. The IRS emphasizes that claiming business-at-home deductions does not automatically trigger an audit on your tax return.

Even so, it is always wise to keep meticulously within the proper guidelines, and of course keep detailed records if you claim business related
expenses when you are working out of your home. You should discuss this aspect of your operation with your tax preparer or a person qualified in the field of small business tax requirements.

If your business earnings aren't subject to withholding tax, and your estimated federal taxes are $100 or more, you'll probably be filing a Declaration of Estimated Tax, Form 1040 ES. To complete
this form, you will have to estimate your income for the coming year and also make a computation of the income tax and self-employed tax you will owe.

The self-employment taxes pay for Social Security coverage. If you have a salaried job covered by Social Security, the self-employment tax applies only to that amount of your home business income that, when added to your salary, reaches the current ceiling. When you file your Form 1040-ES, which is due April 15, you must make the first of four equal installment payments on your estimated tax bill.

Another good way to trim taxes is by setting up a Keogh plan or an Individual Retirement Account. With either of these, you can shelter some of your home business income from taxes by investing it for your retirement.

Chapter 10

Million Dollar Rolodex

Million Dollar Rolodex

TRANSPORTATION
Used Trucks/CARS Online

http://gsaauctions.gov/gsaauctions/gsaauctions/

http://www.ebay.com/motors

http://www.uhaul.com/TruckSales/

http://www.usedtrucks.ryder.com/vehicle/Vehicle
Search.aspx?VehicleTypeId=1&VehicleGroupId=3

http://www.penskeusedtrucks.com/truck-
types/light-and-medium-duty/

Parts

http://www.truckchamp.com/

http://www.autopartswarehouse.com/

Million Dollar Rolodex

Bikes & Motorcycles

http://gsaauctions.gov/gsaauctions/aucindx/

http://www.bikesdirect.com/products/used-bikes/?gclid=CLCF0vaDm7kCFYtDMgodzW0AXQ

http://www.overstock.com/Sports-Toys/Cycling/450/cat.html

http://www.nashbar.com/bikes/TopCategories_10053_10052_-1

http://www.bti-usa.com/

http://evosales.com/

COMPUTERS/Office Equipment

http://www.wtsmedia.com/

http://www.laptopplaza.com/

http://www.outletpc.com/

Million Dollar Rolodex

Computer Tool Kits

http://www.dhgate.com/wholesale/computer+repair+tools.html

http://www.aliexpress.com/wholesale/wholesale-repair-computer-tool.html

http://wholesalecomputercables.com/Computer-Repair-Tool-Kit/M/B00006OXGZ.htm

http://www.amazon.com/Wholesale-Computer-Repair-Screwdriver-Insert/dp/B009KV1MM0

http://www.tigerdirect.com/applications/category/category_tlc.asp?CatId=47&name=Computer%20Tools

Computer Parts

http://www.laptopuniverse.com/

http://www.sabcal.com/

other

http://www.nearbyexpress.com/

http://www.commercialbargains.co

http://www.getpaid2workfromhome.com

http://www.boyerblog.com/success-tools

Million Dollar Rolodex

american merchandise liquidators

http://www.amlinc.com/

the closeout club

http://www.thecloseoutclub.com/

RJ discount sales

http://www.rjsks.com/

St louis wholesale

http://www.stlouiswholesale.com/

Wholesale Electronics

http://www.weisd.com/

ana wholesale

http://www.anawholesale.com/

office wholesale

http://www.1-computerdesks.com/

Million Dollar Rolodex

1aaa wholesale merchandise

http://www.1aaawholesalemerchandise.com/

big lots wholesale

http://www.biglotswholesale.com/

More Business Resources

1.   http://www.sba.gov/content/starting-green-business

home based businesses

2.   http://www.sba.gov/content/home-based-business

3.   online businesses

http://www.sba.gov/content/setting-online-business

4.   self employed and independent contractors

http://www.sba.gov/content/self-employed-independent-contractors

5.   minority owned businesses

http://www.sba.gov/content/minority-owned-businesses

Million Dollar Rolodex

6. veteran owned businesses

http://www.sba.gov/content/veteran-service-disabled-veteran-owned

7. woman owned businesses

http://www.sba.gov/content/women-owned-businesses

8. people with disabilities

http://www.sba.gov/content/people-with-disabilities

9. young entrepreneurs

http://www.sba.gov/content/young-entrepreneurs

$10,000

Massive Money Internet Marketing &

Copy Writing & SEO Course &

$1,000 Value Bonus

Internet Marketing Videos

LIBRARY I (Video Training Programs)

1. Product Creation

2. Copy Writing & Payment

3. Auto Responder & Product Download Page

4. How to start a Freelancing business

5. Video Marketing

6. List Building

7. Affiliate Marketing

8. How to Get Massive Web Site Traffic

LIBRARY II (Video Training Programs)

1. Goldmine Government Grants

2. How to Write a Business Plan

3. Secrets to making money on eBay

4. Credit Repair

5. Goal Setting

6. Asset Protection How to Incorporate

$10,000 MegaSized Internet Marketing &

Copy Writing & SEO Course &

$1,000 Value Bonus

Library III

1. SEO SIMPLIFIED PART 1

2. SEO SIMPLIFIED PART 2

3. SEO Private Network Blogs

4. SEO Social Signals

5. SEO Profits

Bonus 1000 Package!

1. Insider Secrets to Government Contracts (PDF)

2. 1000 Books/Guides (text files)

3. Vacation Discounts (text file w/links to discounts)

4. Media Players (3 Software Programs)

100% MONEY BACK GUARANTEE!!!

ALL ON A 8 GIGABYTE FLASH DRIVE

This Massive Library with a $10,000 value all for only a
1 time payment of $67!!!
Get Instant Access by Using the Link Below:

https://urlzs.com/p7v3T

Leave a review and join Our VIP Mailing List Then Get All our Audio Books Free! We will be releasing over 100 money making audio books within the next 12 months! Just leave a review and join our mailing list and get them all for free!

Just Hit/Type in the Link Below

https://urlzs.com/HfbGF

www.ingramcontent.com/pod-product-compliance
Lightning Source LLC
Chambersburg PA
CBHW061048220326
41597CB00018BA/2621